When The
Paycheck Stops
The
Purpose Begins

*A 21–Day Guided Journal for Women
Ready to Rewrite Your Story*

WILLA ROBINSON

KP PUBLISHING COMPANY

ISBN 978-1-960001-98-6 (Paperback)
ISBN: 978-1-960001-99-3 (eBook)

Library of Congress Control Number: Pending
Editor: Manuscript Mender
Cover Design: Mrs. Gift Osakwe
Literary Director: Sandra Slayton James

Published by:

KP Publishing Company
Publisher of Fiction, Nonfiction & Children's Books
Los Angeles · Las Vegas
www.kp-pub.com

Printed in the United States of America

Dedication

I dedicate this book to the more than **380,000+**
African American women who have recently lost their jobs. May these
pages remind you that even in the midst of uncertainty, purpose still
lives, faith still works, and God is still writing your story.

A Heart Note from Willa

And we know that God causes everything to work together for the good of those who love God and are called according to His purpose for them."

— Romans 8:28 (NIV)

At seventy-seven years old, I can say with confidence, it's true. God really does weave all things together for good. Even when I couldn't see it, He was working behind the scenes, turning pain into purpose and purpose into peace.

When I heard that more than 380,000+ African American women had lost their jobs, my heart ached. I thought about the fear, the grief, and the questions that follow such a sudden change. I asked God, *"How do they recover?"*

And within days, I heard Him answer softly: *"Write the journal."*

When the Paycheck Stops: Purpose Begins is my act of obedience, and my offering of hope. It's for every woman standing at the edge of uncertainty, wondering if she'll ever find her way again.

I want you to know that you're not alone. Even now, in this season, **God is working it together for your good.**

So as you begin these 21 days, take a deep breath and let those words settle into your spirit. You are loved. You are called. And your story is far from over.

With love and purpose,

Willa Robinson

Introduction

From My Heart to Yours

Dear Sister,

If you're holding this journal, I already know two things about you: you've experienced a sudden change that caught you off guard, and deep down, you're still standing because purpose won't let you quit.

Purpose has a way of showing up in the pauses. I didn't plan to write this journal, but when God whispered, 'Write it,' I realized that purpose doesn't stop when circumstances change; it only shifts its form.

Maybe your job ended. Your business may have slowed down. The career you once built with pride no longer feels like home. Whatever brought you here, I want you to know this truth: *the paycheck may have stopped, but your purpose has not.*

You are not alone in this journey. More than 380,000+ Black women have lost jobs in recent months; strong, educated, professional women who poured their hearts into careers that didn't always pour back into them. I saw the headlines, but more than that, I saw the hearts behind the numbers. Women like you. Women like me.

During the pandemic, I worked closely with authors who finally had the time to write the book they had always dreamed of writing. What I didn't expect was how many of them stopped short. Some were afraid to promote, afraid to market, scared to be seen. They had written their truth but hesitated to *live* it out loud. That's when I realized that the story doesn't stop at the final word. That's where the journey begins.

This 21-day journal was born out of that realization that every ending is an invitation to start again, and every woman has a story the world needs. Over these next three weeks, I'll walk beside you through reflection, renewal, and rediscovery. You'll release what was, rediscover who you are, and rewrite what's next; one page, one prayer, one promise at a time.

Together, we're not just rewriting our stories; we're rebuilding lives, restoring confidence, and reminding each other that we still win with faith, resilience, and purpose.

Research shows new habits form in 21 days, but even more powerful:

God can transform our hearts in that time, too. These 21 days are structured to help you shift your mindset, stretch your faith, and step into purpose, one day at a time.

Take your time. Be gentle with yourself. Some days will feel heavy; others, like freedom. But every word you write will move you closer to the woman you're becoming.

So grab your pen, or sit down at your computer or laptop, quiet your mind, and meet me on the next page. Let's write our way forward, not back to who we were, but toward who God purposed us to be.

With love, faith, and purpose,

Contents

Section 3. The Step Forward: Walking in Purpose
Embracing Your Calling and Writing Your New Chapter   61

Section One

The Shift: Releasing What Was
Letting Go of the Past
and Accepting the Change

There comes a moment when life as we knew it changes. Sometimes without warning, sometimes without our permission. The routines, titles, and familiar places that once made us feel secure suddenly slip away, and we're left standing in the quiet space between *what was* and *what's next*.

That's where **The Shift** begins.

It's the place of surrender, the holy moment when you stop fighting what's already gone and start trusting what God is doing next. It's not easy, but it's necessary. Before you can write a new story, you have to release the one that no longer serves your purpose.

In these next few days, give yourself permission to grieve what was, to honor the season that has ended, and to believe that even this transition has divine meaning. Let go with grace, not guilt. God isn't finished. He's simply shifting your position to prepare you for what's ahead.

Day 1 — The Wake-Up Call

Scripture

"And we know that in all things God works for the good of those who love Him, who have been called according to His purpose."

— Romans 8:28 (NIV)

The Way Forward

Sometimes change doesn't knock — it kicks the door open. One day, you're checking emails, attending meetings, balancing deadlines, and then suddenly, the paycheck stops. The rhythm that once defined your days falls silent, leaving questions that echo louder than answers.

It's okay to feel disoriented. To grieve. To wonder how something that once seemed so secure could vanish so fast. But maybe this isn't an ending at all — maybe it's a *divine interruption*. A wake-up call inviting you to pause, listen, and rediscover the woman behind the title.

You are not your job, your position, or your last performance review. You are purpose in motion — even now. What feels like loss may be God's invitation to rest, reimagine, and reset your story with Him as the author.

Today is not about finding all the answers. It's about opening your heart to the truth that you're still here — and that means purpose still lives in you.

Writing Prompt:

What emotions surfaced when your professional rhythm changed, and how might God be using this season to redirect your steps?

Power Statement

I may have lost the paycheck, but I have not lost my purpose.

My Next Chapter

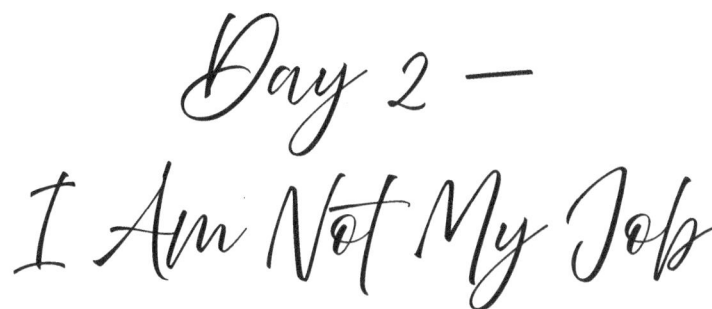

Scripture

"Before I formed you in the womb I knew you; before you were born I set you apart."

— Jeremiah 1:5 (NIV)

The Way Forward

You gave your best to your work: your energy, your commitment, your time, and now it's gone. That kind of shift can shake your sense of who you are. For years, you may have introduced yourself by your title, your company, or your position. But God is whispering: *You are more than what you did.*

Your worth isn't tied to a paycheck, a performance review, or anyone's approval. You are purpose in motion, designed for impact beyond a job description. This pause is not punishment; it's preparation.

It's a divine opportunity to rediscover who you are without the name badge.

Today, stand tall in your true identity—not as an employee, but as a daughter of purpose, equipped and anointed for what's next.

Writing Prompt

What qualities, gifts, or values
define who you are beyond your career?

Power Statement

My identity is not my position—my value comes from my purpose.

My Next Chapter

When the Paycheck Stops The Purpose Begins

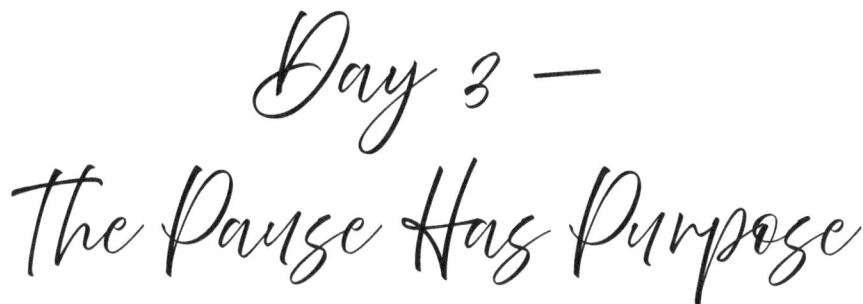

Day 3 —
The Pause Has Purpose

Scripture

"The Lord will fight for you; you need only to be still."

— Exodus 14:14 (NIV)

The Way Forward

Silence after the storm can feel unbearable. When the daily rush stops, your thoughts grow louder, which can be uncomfortable. But what if the stillness is sacred? What if this pause is God's protection, pulling you aside to prepare you for greater?

Purpose often grows in quiet places. This season isn't wasted; it's working for you. There's something divine happening in the delay; a reset, a redirection, a revelation. God uses pauses to restore perspective, reorder priorities, and remind you that your pace was never meant to outrun your peace.

Instead of fighting the stillness, breathe it in. There's purpose in your pause, and strength in your surrender.

Writing Prompt

What might God be teaching you in this quiet space
between endings and new beginnings?

Power Statement

The pause is not punishment. It's preparation for my next purpose.

My Next Chapter

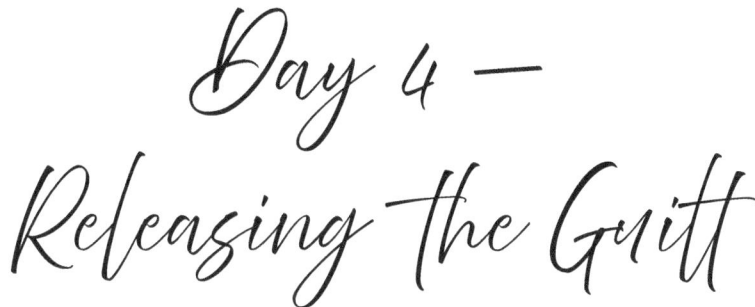

Day 4 — Releasing the Guilt

Scripture

"Therefore, there is now no condemnation for those who are in Christ Jesus."

— Romans 8:1 (NIV)

The Way Forward

Guilt has a way of clinging to what could've been, "I should've seen it coming," "I could've done more." But guilt doesn't serve your healing; it keeps you tied to a version of yourself that no longer exists. Letting go is not giving up, it's giving God permission to rewrite the story.

You did your best with what you knew then. Now, grace is inviting you to release the weight of self-blame and trust that even your mistakes have been woven into your mission. Freedom begins when you forgive yourself for being human.

Today, lay guilt down at the altar of grace. You can't move forward carrying what was never meant for your shoulders.

Writing Prompt

What guilt or regret are you ready
to release so that healing can begin?

Power Statement

I let go of guilt and embrace grace. I am free to move forward.

My Next Chapter

_____

_____

_____

_____

_____

_____

_____

_____

_____

_____

_____

_____

_____

_____

_____

_____

_____

Day 5 —
When Faith Feels Fragile

Scripture

"Even when I walk through the darkest valley, I will not be afraid, for You are close beside me."

— Psalm 23:4 (NLT)

The Way Forward

There are days when even the strongest woman wonders if God still hears her. You've prayed, you've waited, and still silence. That silence can shake the faith you thought was unshakable. But even fragile faith is *faith*.

When everything familiar falls away, faith doesn't mean pretending you're OK. It means trusting God when you're not. It's OK to admit that belief feels hard. God isn't offended by your questions; He's drawn to your truth, your integrity. Faith grows in the cracks of uncertainty, watered by tears and persistence.

Today, I ask you to hold on, not to how things were, but to the One who holds your future. Sometimes, we have to send up a quick prayer several times a day, *"Help me, Lord. I trust in you."* Faith doesn't always roar; sometimes it just whispers, and He answers, *"Keep going."*

Writing Prompt

When has your faith felt fragile, and what helped you
keep believing through that season?

Power Statement

Even when my faith feels small, God's strength in me is unbreakable.

My Next Chapter

Day 6 —
Counting Hidden Blessings

Scripture

"Give thanks in all circumstances; for this is God's will for you in Christ Jesus."

— 1 Thessalonians 5:18 (NIV)

The Way Forward

It's easy to see blessings when life is full, but harder when things feel empty. Yet God's grace often shows up quietly in the friend who checks in, the bill that's somehow paid, the peace that makes no sense at all. These are not coincidences; they are confirmations that you're still covered.

Gratitude doesn't ignore pain; it reframes it. It reminds you that even in loss, there's something left to thank God for. Every breath, every sunrise, every act of kindness is proof that He hasn't forgotten you.

Today, look beyond what ended and notice what remains. Gratitude is the bridge between heartbreak and healing.

Writing Prompt

What hidden blessings or quiet provisions have
reminded you that you are still seen and supported?

Power Statement

Gratitude shifts my focus from what ended to what remains.

My Next Chapter

_____

_____

_____

_____

_____

_____

_____

_____

_____

_____

_____

_____

_____

_____

_____

_____

_____

_____

When the Paycheck Stops The Purpose Begins

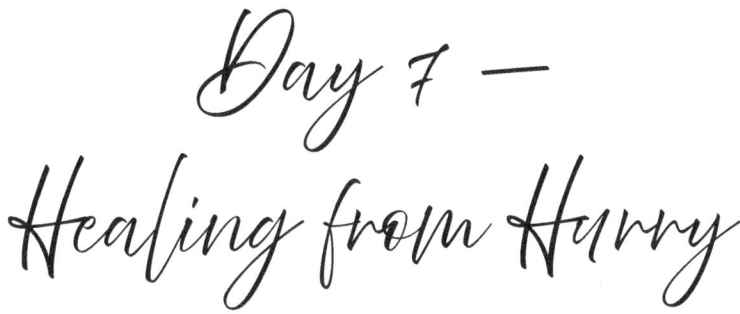

Day 7 —
Healing from Hurry

Scripture

"Come to Me, all you who are weary and burdened, and I will give you rest."

— Matthew 11:28 (NIV)

The Way Forward

For years, you moved fast; proving, producing, performing. Now God is inviting you to a slower, sacred rhythm. Healing can't be rushed; it unfolds in stillness. When the calendar clears and the inbox goes quiet, you may feel lost, but this unhurried space is holy ground.

Sometimes, slowing down is how we speed up in purpose. God is doing deep work beneath the surface. He's mending what hustle broke, restoring what busyness buried. Let the pace of peace become your new productivity.

Today, give yourself permission to rest without guilt. You are not falling behind; you are being rebuilt.

Writing Prompt

How can you practice rest and stillness
this week as part of your healing journey?

Power Statement

Rest is not weakness. It's God's way of rebuilding my strength.

My Next Chapter

_____

_____

_____

_____

_____

_____

_____

_____

_____

_____

_____

_____

_____

_____

_____

Section Two

The Stretch: Trusting What's Unseen
Building Faith and Confidence
for What's Next

Once you've released what was, God begins to stretch you toward what can be. It's the in-between, where faith meets uncertainty and growth begins.

Stretching doesn't always feel good. It asks you to believe before you see, to walk before you know the destination. But this is where you start to strengthen your spiritual muscles: faith, trust, courage, and obedience.

In this section, you'll learn to lean into God's promises instead of your plans. Each day will challenge you to think differently, to pray deeper, and to remember that even in the stretching, God is steady.

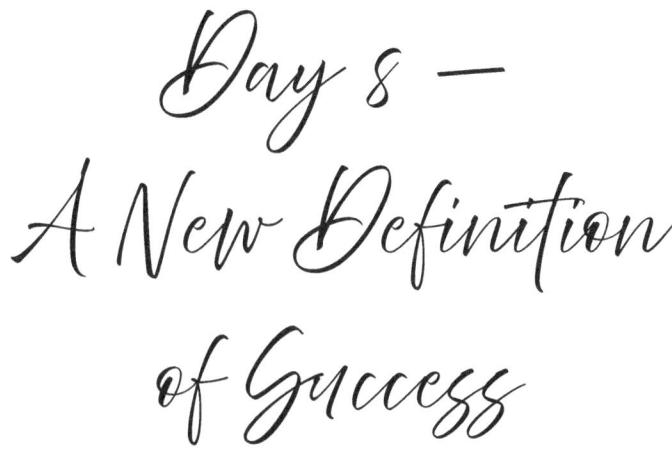

Day 8 —
A New Definition
of Success

Scripture

"Commit to the Lord whatever you do, and He will establish your plans."

— Proverbs 16:3 (NIV)

The Way Forward

For years, success was measured by promotions, titles, and the size of a paycheck. But now, in the stillness, God invites you to redefine it. True success isn't found in performance; it's found in peace. It's walking in obedience, even when the next step isn't obvious.

Success, in God's language, is *alignment.* It's doing what He asks, when He asks, and trusting the outcome to Him. Sometimes success looks like starting over; other times it's simply standing still and believing again.

Today, release the pressure to prove yourself. Let your new measure of success be faithfulness, not busyness; purpose, not position.

Writing Prompt

What would your life look like if "success" meant walking
in peace instead of chasing perfection?

Power Statement

My success is measured by my obedience to God's purpose for me.

My Next Chapter

When the Paycheck Stops The Purpose Begins

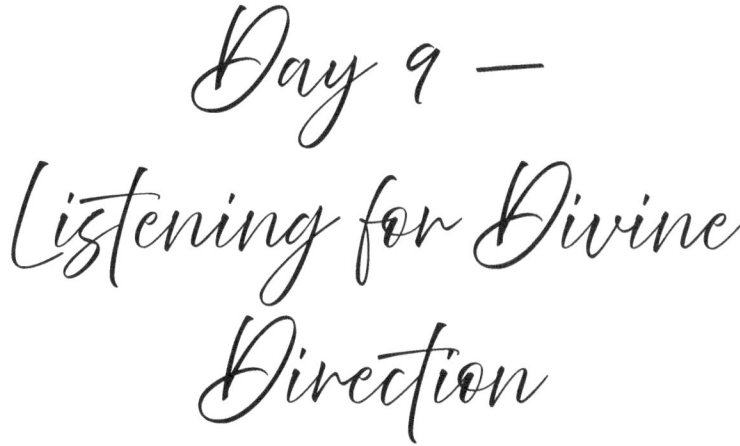

Day 9 — Listening for Divine Direction

Scripture

"Your ears shall hear a word behind you, saying, 'This is the way, walk in it,' when you turn to the right hand or when you turn to the left."

— Isaiah 30:21 (NKJV)

The Way Forward

The world tells you to move faster, do more, but God often speaks in whispers. His guidance rarely shouts; it settles softly in your spirit. When everything familiar disappears, His voice becomes the compass that leads you forward.

Sometimes direction doesn't come as a map but as a moment; a nudge, a phrase in prayer, a verse that won't leave your mind. Divine direction is less about rushing toward answers and more about resting in awareness. God is the best navigator we will ever have. Let Him provide the direction, and I guarantee you will arrive at your destination safely and on time.

Today, create quiet. Turn down the noise of worry and doubt. God is still speaking, not in confusion, but in clarity born of peace.

Writing Prompt

When have you sensed God guiding you through
subtle signs, whispers, or moments of peace?

Power Statement

God's voice leads me with clarity, calm, and confidence.

My Next Chapter

_____

_____

_____

_____

_____

_____

_____

_____

_____

_____

_____

_____

_____

_____

_____

_____

Day 10 —
Unpacking Your Gifts

Scripture

"Each of you should use whatever gift you have received to serve others, as faithful stewards of God's grace in its various forms."

— 1 Peter 4:10 (NIV)

The Way Forward

Buried beneath busyness are the gifts God placed in you long before your first job. They didn't vanish with a layoff or title change; they're waiting to be rediscovered. Purpose doesn't start with employment; it starts with *empowerment*.

Your gifts were never meant to hide behind someone else's vision. They're divine tools designed for your unique assignment. When you recognize what God placed in your hands, you stop asking for permission to shine.

Today, take inventory. What comes naturally? What makes your heart light up? Those are clues to your calling—gifts that, when offered back to God, create impact beyond paychecks and promotions.

Writing Prompt

What abilities or passions feel most alive in you,
and how could they serve others in this new season?

Power Statement

*My gifts are divine tools, and I choose to use them
with purpose and joy.*

My Next Chapter

Day 11 —
Courage To Dream Again

Scripture

"Now to Him who is able to do immeasurably more than all we ask or imagine, according to His power that is at work within us."

— Ephesians 3:20 (NIV)

The Way Forward

When life disappoints you, dreams can feel dangerous. It's safer not to hope too big, not to believe too boldly. But the God who gave you vision hasn't changed His mind. The detour didn't cancel your destiny; it refined it.

Dreaming again takes courage, the courage to believe that "different" can still be good, that "later" doesn't mean "never." God's imagination for you is still unfolding. Let Him stretch your faith beyond what you think is possible. I had no idea I would be writing this journal until **September 3, 2025**. I had just heard that more than 300,000 African American women had lost their jobs, and my heart sank. I remember asking God, *"How do they recover?"*

Two or three days later, I heard Him speak clearly: *"Write the journal."*

That moment changed everything. What started as a question became a calling. What began as a concern turned into an assignment. And now, here we are, walking this 21-day journey together, reminding one another that even when life shifts, faith still stands.

Today, dare to dream with God again. Not small, safe dreams, but bold, beautiful ones rooted in purpose.

Writing Prompt

What dream have you buried out of fear or disappointment,
and what would it take to believe in it again?

Power Statement

My dreams are alive in God's hands,
and I have the courage to believe again.

My Next Chapter

When the Paycheck Stops The Purpose Begins

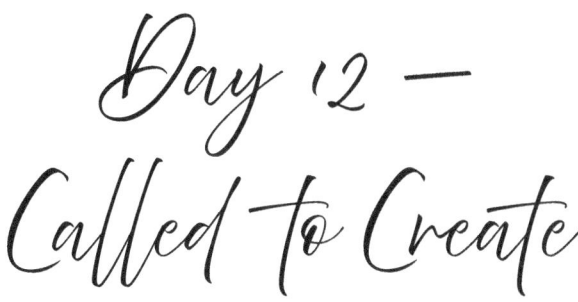

Day 12 — Called to Create

Scripture

"We are God's masterpiece. He has created us anew in Christ Jesus, so we can do the good things He planned for us long ago."

— Ephesians 2:10 (NLT)

The Way Forward

Inside you is a creative spark that refuses to fade. It's the part of you that writes, paints, cooks, builds, sings, or dreams solutions no one else sees. Creativity is not a luxury. It's a reflection of your Creator.

God designed you to bring something new into the world. When you create, you partner with Him in healing and renewal. Don't minimize your gift because it doesn't fit someone else's mold. Your creativity is your ministry.

Today, honor that spark. Give it space, give it breath, and let God use it to remind you that you were made to create. And as my pastor's wife, Lady Sandra Harris, recently preached in a message that touched my heart, *"You Were Built for This."*

Built for resilience. Built for faith. Built for purpose. Built to bring forth something only you can give the world.

Writing Prompt

What creative expressions bring you joy, and how can you use them to bless others in this season?

Power Statement

My creativity reflects the Creator,
and I will use it with freedom and faith.

My Next Chapter

_____

_____

_____

_____

_____

_____

_____

_____

_____

_____

_____

_____

_____

_____

_____

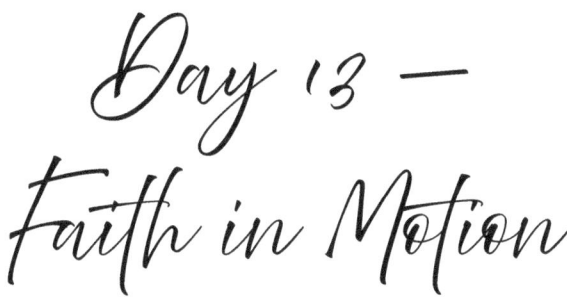

Day 13 — Faith in Motion

Scripture

"Show me your faith without your deeds, and I will show you my faith by my deeds."

— James 2:18 (NIV)

The Way Forward

Faith isn't just what you feel; it's what you *do*. It's the courage to act when you can't yet see the outcome. God moves through movement. Each small step becomes a declaration that you trust His plan more than your comfort.

Start where you are with what you have. Write the first page, make the call, send the email, enroll in the class. Action breathes life into faith.

Today, take one simple step toward your next chapter. You don't need the whole plan, just the willingness to begin.

Writing Prompt

What is one small action you can take today
that aligns with the purpose God is showing you?

Power Statement

My faith moves me forward, one obedient step at a time.

My Next Chapter

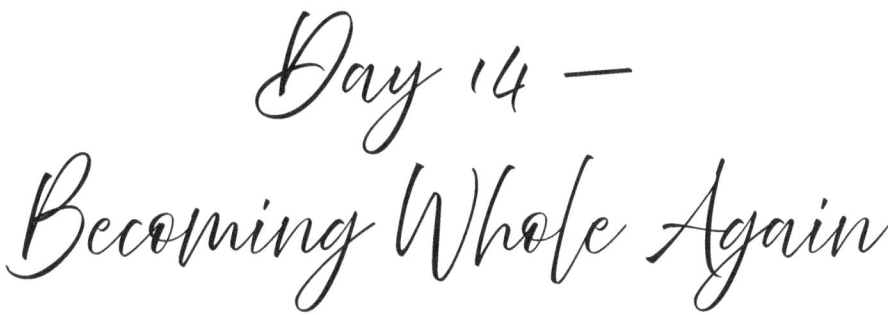

Day 14 —
Becoming Whole Again

Scripture

"He heals the brokenhearted and binds up their wounds."

— Psalm 147:3 (NIV)

The Way Forward

Wholeness doesn't mean everything is perfect; it means you're no longer fragmented by what hurt you. God is piecing you together; gently, lovingly, intentionally. Every scar becomes a story of His restoration.

Becoming whole is a process, not a performance. Learning to love yourself through the rebuilding. You are not behind; you are being refined. Every day you choose hope over fear, forgiveness over bitterness, you heal a little more.

Today, thank God for progress instead of perfection. You are whole, even while you're still healing.

Writing Prompt

What parts of your heart or identity is God restoring in this season?

Power Statement

I am healing, growing, and becoming
whole through God's restoring love.

My Next Chapter

Section Three

The Step Forward: Walking in Purpose
Embracing Your Calling and Writing Your New Chapter

After the releasing and the stretching comes the stepping. It's the moment where faith turns into motion. It's where you begin to live what you've written, to walk boldly in the new story God is unfolding through you.

The Step Forward isn't about rushing ahead; it's about moving with intention and grace. You've faced your fears, strengthened your faith, and rediscovered your voice. Now it's time to use it.

In this section, you'll capture the lessons, dreams, and divine direction that have surfaced during this journey. You'll begin to see that what once felt like loss has become the soil for growth, proof that purpose was waiting all along.

So take the step. You're ready. God's already gone before you.

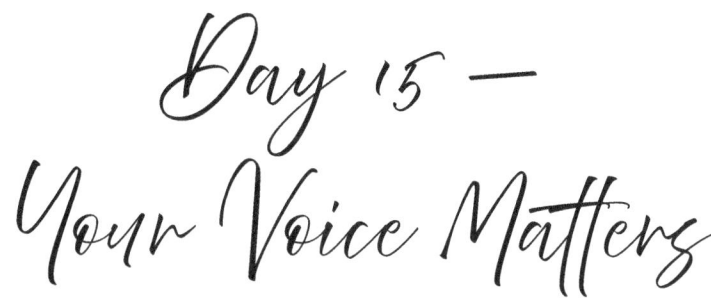

Scripture

"Let the redeemed of the Lord tell their story—those He redeemed from the hand of the enemy."

— Psalm 107:2 (NIV)

The Way Forward

Hear me well, your story carries power, not because it's perfect, but because it's *yours.* Someone needs to hear what you've lived through so they can believe they'll make it through, too. The enemy hopes you'll stay silent, but God is calling you to speak, to write, and to share your truth.

Don't underestimate your testimony. Every trial you've faced holds wisdom that someone else is praying for. Your pain can become a roadmap for another woman's breakthrough.

Today, say it out loud: *The enemy will not keep me silent. My voice matters.* Then, write what you once tried to forget. Healing happens when honesty finds a home on paper.

Writing Prompt

What part of your story are you being nudged
to share so that it can help someone else heal?

Power Statement

My story has power, and my voice is a vessel of healing.

My Next Chapter

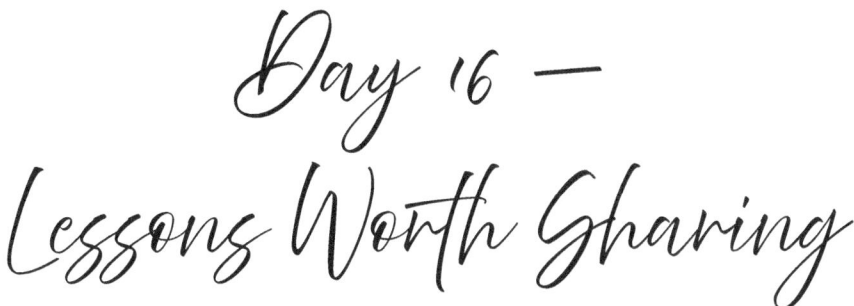

Day 16 —
Lessons Worth Sharing

Scripture

"And we know that in all things God works for the good of those who love Him, who have been called according to His purpose."

— Romans 8:28 (NIV)

The Way Forward

When you start to write, every chapter of your life, even the hard ones, carries a lesson worth sharing. God wastes nothing. The very thing you thought disqualified you might be the reason someone else finds hope.

Take time to look back not with regret, but with gratitude for the growth. You've learned resilience, faith, and wisdom that textbooks can't teach. Those lessons are treasures you can now offer to others.

And guess what, as long as you are on this earth, there will be lessons learned.

Today, honor your experiences by writing them down. What God brought you through wasn't random — it was preparation for purpose.

Writing Prompt

What life lessons has God taught you through challenges
that you can now use to encourage others?

Power Statement

Every lesson I've learned carries purpose,
and I will use it to uplift others.

My Next Chapter

_____

_____

_____

_____

_____

_____

_____

_____

_____

_____

_____

_____

_____

_____

_____

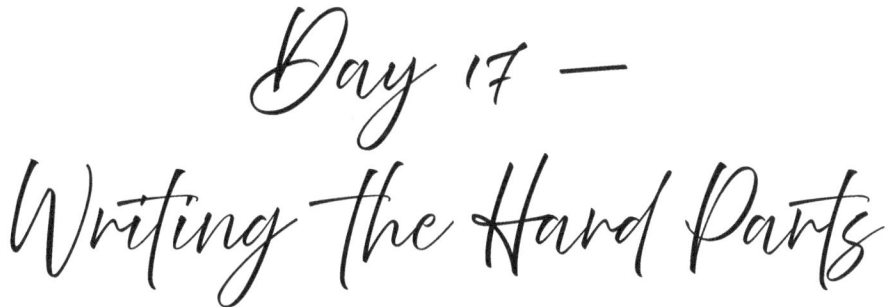

Day 17 — Writing the Hard Parts

Scripture

"You intended to harm me, but God intended it for good to accomplish what is now being done."

— Genesis 50:20 (NIV)

The Way Forward

Some stories are hard to tell because they still ache when you touch them. But healing lives in honesty. When you write the hard parts, you take back the power of what once tried to break you.

Your story isn't defined by pain but by perseverance. God doesn't erase the hard chapters; He redeems them. As you write, remember, this isn't about reliving the hurt; it's about reclaiming your strength.

Today, be brave enough to tell the truth. Someone's freedom is waiting on your transparency.

Writing Prompt

What painful experience is God inviting you to write about so it can become part of your healing and someone else's hope?

Power Statement

My truth is not my shame—it's my testimony.

My Next Chapter

Day 18 — The Legacy Shift

Scripture

"Write the vision and make it plain."

— Habakkuk 2:2 (KJV)

The Way Forward

What is Legacy? It isn't just what you leave behind.

It's what you live right now. Every word you write, every person you encourage, every prayer you whisper becomes part of the story you'll be remembered for.

You're not too late to start shaping your legacy. God doesn't measure time; He measures obedience. As you walk in purpose, your life becomes a message that outlives the moment.

Today, write with legacy in mind. What will your story say about faith, perseverance, and purpose?

Writing Prompt

What kind of legacy do you want your life and story to leave behind?

Power Statement

My legacy is one of faith, purpose, and perseverance.

My Next Chapter

Day 19 —
Standing in Purpose

Scripture

"For we are co-workers in God's service."

— 1 Corinthians 3:9 (NIV)

The Way Forward

You've done the inner work; now it's time to stand. Purpose isn't passive; it's an active partnership with God. It's stepping into opportunities, conversations, and callings that align with who you're becoming.

Standing in purpose means no longer apologizing for your anointing. You've prayed through pain and persevered through pressure; now it's time to shine with intention.

Today, take up space as a woman of faith and vision. You are God's partner in purpose; stand firm in that truth.

Writing Prompt

What does it look like for you to walk confidently
in your purpose today?

Power Statement

I no longer shrink back — I stand fully in my purpose.

My Next Chapter

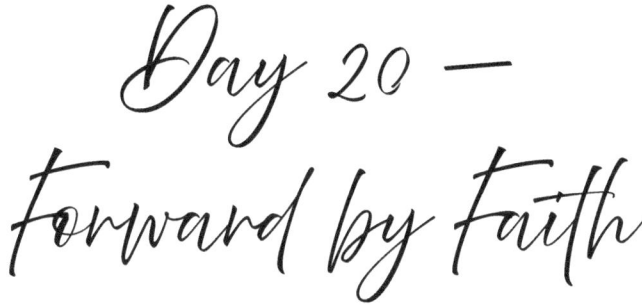

Day 20 —
Forward by Faith

Scripture

"For we walk by faith, not by sight."

— 2 Corinthians 5:7 (NKJV)

The Way Forward

Faith doesn't erase uncertainty; it transforms it. Walking by faith means trusting that God's plan will make sense in time, even when it doesn't right now. The path ahead might not be clear, but your steps are ordered.

You've seen what happens when you try to control outcomes. Now, let peace be your strategy. Move forward knowing that every unknown is known to Him.

Today, choose faith over fear, again and again, until forward becomes your rhythm.

Writing Prompt

What area of your life requires you to walk by faith
rather than rely on what you can see?

Power Statement

I choose faith over fear, trusting God with every step forward.

My Next Chapter

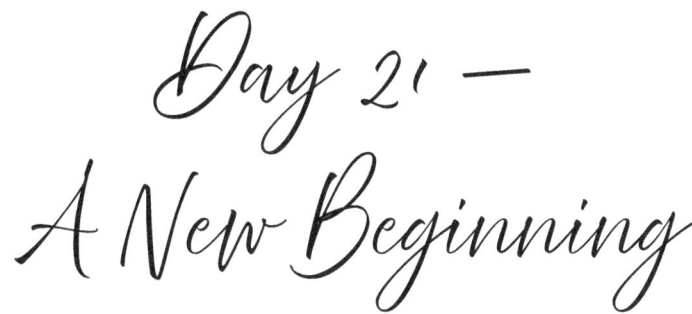

Day 21 — A New Beginning

Scripture

"Behold, I am doing a new thing! Now it springs up; do you not perceive it?"

— Isaiah 43:19 (NIV)

The Way Forward

You've shown immense courage and strength in coming through loss, rediscovered your gifts, and found the courage to dream again. Now, you stand on the threshold of something new, not the life you had, but the life God created for you.

New beginnings don't erase the past; they redeem it. Everything you've endured, every tear shed, every moment of waiting, every step of healing, all of it was necessary to birth what's next.

Today, lift your head, open your heart, and walk boldly into your new beginning. You've been preparing for this, and now, you're ready. Purpose is calling, and you're ready.

Writing Prompt

What does "new" look like for you,
and how will you walk into it with confidence and faith?

Power Statement

I am walking boldly into my new beginning —
purpose, peace, and promise await me.

My Next Chapter

Understanding the Grief of Job Loss

Healing Through Faith, Grace, and Self-Compassion

Losing a job can feel like losing a part of your identity, your rhythm, or even your security. It's more than a professional setback; it's an emotional experience that can stir feelings of fear, anger, sadness, and uncertainty.

Just as we grieve after the loss of a loved one, we can also grieve when the structure and stability of our work life suddenly change. The good news is that **grief is not the end of your story—it's the doorway to transformation.**

As you move through this journey, remember that **God is present in every stage**. His plan is still at work, even when you can't yet see it.

The Five Stages of Grief
(Adapted from the Kübler-Ross model and applied to job loss)

1. Denial – "This can't be happening."

You may feel numb or disconnected at first, struggling to believe your situation is real. It's your mind's way of protecting you from emotional overload.

> *"The Lord is close to the brokenhearted and saves those who are crushed in spirit."*
>
> — Psalm 34:18 (NIV)

Give yourself permission to feel what you feel. Healing begins when we stop pretending we're not hurting.

2. Anger – "Why me?"

Anger can arise toward an employer, coworkers, or even yourself. Don't suppress it; acknowledge it and bring it to God.

> *"Be angry, and do not sin; meditate within your heart on your bed, and be still."*
>
> — Psalm 4:4 (NKJV)

Anger can be fuel — let God transform it into determination and direction.

3. Bargaining – "If only I had . . ."

You may replay events or wish you'd done something differently. These thoughts reflect your desire for control in a moment that felt out of your hands.

> *"Trust in the Lord with all your heart and lean not on your own understanding."*
> — Proverbs 3:5 (NIV)

Release the "what ifs." God's plan is still unfolding — and nothing is wasted.

4. Depression – "What's the point now?"

This is often the hardest stage. Sadness, fatigue, or hopelessness may set in. You are not weak for feeling this way; you are human.

> *"He heals the brokenhearted and binds up their wounds."*
> — Psalm 147:3 (NIV)

Remember: this season is temporary. Light is coming — and your purpose still stands.

5. Acceptance – "It happened. Now what?"

Acceptance isn't about liking what happened. It's about understanding that life continues, and God still has a plan for you. In acceptance, there's peace, readiness, and a stirring of new purpose.

> *"Behold, I am doing a new thing; now it springs forth—do you not perceive it?"*
>
> — Isaiah 43:19 (ESV)

Acceptance opens the door for divine redirection.

Moving Forward

Healing is not linear. You may revisit these stages in different ways, and that's okay. Let journaling, prayer, and community be your companions on this journey.

You are not alone.
God is not done.
Your story is still being written — with grace, faith, and purpose guiding every word.

> *"Weeping may endure for a night, but joy comes in the morning."*
>
> — Psalm 30:5 (NKJV)

My Next Chapter

Acknowledgments

"To God be the glory, great things He has done."

— Psalm 126:3

With a grateful heart, first, I give all honor and glory to God for giving me the idea, the inspiration, and the words to write this journal. Every page is a reflection of His grace and faithfulness.

To my sons, **Vernon and Raymond**, my sister, **Mollie**, and my brother, **Ben**—thank you from the bottom of my heart for always being willing to accept my interruptions and listen to my endless ideas, podcasts, Bible verses, and whatever else God places on my heart. Words are not enough to fully express my love and appreciation for each of you.

To my church family, **Pastor Daryl Harris, Lady Sandra Harris**, and the entire congregation of Bethesda Church of God in Christ, North Las Vegas, Nevada. Thank you for surrounding me with love, prayer, and spiritual strength. Your love, kindness, teaching, and genuine fellowship renew my soul every time I enter those doors. You have not only encouraged me; you have anchored me.

To my **editor, cover designer, and interior designer**, thank you for the excellence, creativity, and dedication you poured into this work. Teamwork truly is everything, and I know I could not have done this without your skill, patience, and partnership. I thank God for placing you in my path.

About the Author

For more than seventeen years, **Willa Robinson** has dedicated her life to helping others bring their stories to life. As CEO and Publisher of **KP Publishing Company**, she has guided countless first-time authors through the writing and publishing process, empowering them to share their experiences, wisdom, and testimonies with excellence and impact.

Willa believes deeply that every person has a story that matters — a story God can use to heal, inspire, teach, and transform lives. She has built her company on the foundation of **faith, integrity, and community**, ensuring that underrepresented voices receive the support they deserve.

After decades of coaching and publishing books for others, Willa now brings that same passion and calling to her own writing. *When the Paycheck Stops, the Purpose Begins* is a mission — it is her heart for women in transition. It is her response to the staggering number of professional Black women who have experienced job loss and identity disruption during recent years.

Her mission is to remind women that:
Their purpose is not defined by a job title
Their voice is a gift that must not be silenced
Their story is powerful and worth writing

As a woman of faith who has overcome profound personal challenges, Willa knows the strength it takes to keep believing when circumstances shift unexpectedly. She stands as a testament that **purpose lives on the other side of pain** — and that God's plan always extends beyond any paycheck.

Through publishing, coaching, speaking, and now this national movement, Willa is committed to helping women rediscover hope, rebuild confidence, and **write their next chapter with purpose**.

Willa is the proud mother of two adult sons, Vernon and Raymond, daughter-in-law, Micole, three granddaughters, Ashlee, Sharae, and Maleah, one grandson, Miles, and one great-grandson, Amir. She resides in Las Vegas, Nevada.

www.ingramcontent.com/pod-product-compliance
Lightning Source LLC
Chambersburg PA
CBHW051322120626
46547CB00015B/2355